WHEN RAPE BECOMES ACCEPTABLE

Corrective Rape in Jamaica

WHEN RAPE BECOMES ACCEPTABLE

Kemone S-G Brown

TAMARiND HiLL
.PRESS

Acknowledgement

I am forever grateful to the women who entrusted me with something so personal and painful to them. You have all opened up my world in a way that I never imagined possible. Your individual strength has taught me that survival is inevitable for the female. Thank you for allowing me to share your stories with the world, because I know it will make a difference for someone somewhere.

To my father, George, I really could not have finished this project without you. Thank you so much; for always holding me accountable, for your continued support and endless encouragement. You remind me *often* that I had a job to do and it wasn't yet completed. You taught me the importance of keeping a promise and made sure I kept the promise I made to all these women to bring this issue to the forefront. I am forever grateful.

The women at Female Oxygen, made it possible to garner the resources I needed to publish this work; from me and the women represented in this book as well as all the other lives that will be affected, thank you for your selfless giving.

Thanks to my confidante Rosanna, who supported me through the darkest of times, helping me to gather the strength I needed to finish this work and gave valuable input into this project. My mother, sisters and brother must also be thanked for helping me to get back on track and finish this project. Thank you all for pulling me together when I needed you the most and for your individual support, love and encouragement.

Thank you to my sister and Editor Tashana. Over the last few years you have helped me on this journey in more ways than one. Your advice, skills, belief in me and support has helped me to bring this to life.

Thanks to everyone who was there to inspire and support me when I wanted to throw in the towel. To those who were there to help me work through the pain, confusion and doubts, words cannot begin to express my gratitude.

And to my sister Saun-Jaye, thanks for reminding me of my internal strength.

Preface

I stumbled upon this project by accident. As a human rights activist with a natural hunger for knowledge, I was interested in understanding HIV and AIDs in the lesbian and bisexual women community in Jamaica. In different circles, I had heard several arguments on the topic, some of which seemed plausible, but none of it were facts. There were no books or dissertations to read on HIV and AIDs in the non-heterosexual women community in Jamaica and I was curious. Naturally, the more I heard the more I questioned the facts around the issue and wanted to learn more. I wasn't comfortable with hearing the assumptions being made by anyone, especially those that were accusatory, blaming or just showed total disregard on the matter. I wanted to find the facts and so I went in search of them.

In 2007, I developed a study for which I later presented the findings at the 5th Asia and Pacific Conference on Reproductive and Sexual Health and Rights (APCRSHR) in Beijing towards the end of 2009. For this study, I managed to get lesbian and bisexual women, some I met for the first time, to confide in me about how they had contracted the disease. Some of the findings of the study took me by surprise. One in particular was the fact that a few of the women disclosed that they had contracted the virus through rape. It wasn't the 'rape' I was <u>familiar</u> with; these women were raped because they were lesbians or bisexual. For the first time, I learned about the existence of "corrective rape" in our society. At the time of the study and hearing the stories of the women I didn't know the term "corrective rape". I was cognisant of the fact that rape had always been a weapon of war used to weaken women and girls, but I didn't realise that men in our society had declared war on the bodies of lesbian and bisexual women because of their sexual orientation or at least not in that way.

It wasn't until I was having discussions with fellow activists at a conference in Cape Town, that I realised that this was an issue not just affecting Jamaican lesbian and bisexual women; it was an issue facing lesbians in many countries. It was on that trip in

2008 that I learned the term "corrective rape" a term coined by South Africans that defined the raping of women to conform them to heterosexuality or to "cure" them. I knew then that this was something I needed to understand more. Rape itself was something I struggled to grasp and this wasn't easier. I couldn't comprehend how a man thought that by raping lesbian and bisexual women it would "make them straight"; that they would realise while being tortured and violated, that they were suddenly heterosexuals.

Close to the end of 2008 I returned to Jamaica to collect data for this new project. With no idea of where it would lead me, I started on this journey. I simply wanted to know how the women knew the difference between being *simply raped* and being a victim of corrective rape: the victim of a hate crime. I wanted to know how it affected their lives and how they got justice. I wanted corrective rape to be something that we were talking about and fighting against as we were any other forms of rape. In my opinion, it was as important as any other forms of war on women's bodies the feminist movement was fighting against, yet it wasn't on the agenda.

In my report at the 5th APCSRHR I spoke on the matter only briefly; firstly due to my lack of understanding on the subject matter and secondly because I was presenting my study on HIV and AIDs in lesbian and bisexual women. By this time, I had in my possession, data taken in interviews from women about being raped because of their sexual orientation. Having this information was one thing but I fully understood that I couldn't get justice for the women who I soon realised had no recourse or were riddled with shame and fear; so much so that they didn't want to be known. They were willing to share their stories but didn't want anyone to know it was theirs. Their perspective was that *the idea of getting justice in Jamaica on any issue was faint, and people island wide were suffering in silence so they weren't very different.* I accepted their perspectives and their decisions. But I needed to find a way to bring this issue to the forefront.

The idea of the book came to me in 2009 after picking my brain for months trying to figure out how to bring the issue to light without '_outing_' the women. However, for the next few years I struggled with bringing the book to life. There were a huge number of challenges in completing the project. The greatest by far was having to revisit the interviews and witness each and every time, what each woman had been through, is still going through. I've learned through their stories that it is not something one gets over.

This project was bigger than I thought, finding the right way to present the information was not an easy task. Over the years I continued to baffle with the question; how do I expose the issue without exposing the women? It took many attempts and a lot of energy; often I just wanted to give up. Then finally, after attempting, completing, and abandoning the project twice due to not being satisfied with the final product, I revisited it one final time and this book was born.

This collection of short stories captures the horrible experiences of women who were victims of hate manifested through physical harm; rape and violence. Their stories are profound and more than thought provoking. While these women do not want to be known, their stories are evidence of the vicious crime that continues to go unpunished not just in Jamaica but in other countries as well. These are just a few of the many stories that exist. Lesbian and bisexual women continue to suffer in silence.

Hopefully in the future we will see progress being made in tackling this issue globally.

Lashaun

Lashaun had spent the entire day laying building blocks. She was no mason, but quite muscular and known to be very strong; masons in her community would take her on a building site every now and then. Being a high school dropout, she didn't have a steady job and would take whatever little jobs came her way. Like many other Jamaicans in her position, she needed to feed herself and did whatever work brought the cash in.

Looking in, she appeared to be the typical tomboy. Few people knew, that under the extremely baggy shirts and jeans was a 'bikini bod'. She was amazingly curvaceous. Her mother thought she'd become a model and go on to be Miss Jamaica World, but that was nowhere in the dreams and plans Lashaun had for herself. She wanted to be an architect and other than her girlfriends she wasn't comfortable with anyone seeing her curves.

Originally from West Kingston, Lashaun had spent most of her later years down South where the woman she had fallen in love with was from. This according to Lashaun was quite dangerous as she was not originated from South Kingston and was thus seen as an outcast. However, her girlfriend continuously assured her that she'd face no harm. Princess, Lashaun's girlfriend, was an exotic dancer in a popular night club in New Kingston. She spent most of the day sleeping as she worked nights and would only return home at around five or six each morning. Princess' job was more stable, hence the move down South. The two were somewhat routine. Lashaun would walk Princess to the main road to grab a taxi around 9:30pm each evening. She would return home, turn the TV on, watch a movie or something, and then fall asleep after midnight after Princess' final check in for the night. Somewhere between five and six the following morning Princess would return home. When Lashaun didn't have to work, Princess would join her in bed. Lashaun would awake late morning and prepare breakfast. They'd spend the rest of the day doing random things. When Lashaun had work she was out of bed by 5am and would be out the door as Princess was coming in.

Members of the community speculated as to the nature of their relationship and it wasn't long before they had hit the nail right on the head. They were constantly called names and received random threats. Lashaun being the introvert and un-confrontational person, wanted to move as soon as she heard the threats.

"Princess, what if they shoot me?" she had worriedly questioned her girlfriend.

"Gal stop the nonsense, people just talk as they have a right. It will soon blow over." Princess had laughed it off.

5

Though she didn't say, Lashaun was scared for her life. After all, she was an outsider. For the next few weeks Lashaun would pretend she was jogging on her way from helping Princess to her taxi. She just wanted to stay out of danger and that, for her meant staying off the street. When she was in the house she would make sure the few windows and doors were locked tight. She kept the TV on low so she could hear the slightest movement outside and slept with a machete under her bed and an ice-pick under her pillow. She was prepared to fight for her life if the need presented itself. When she left for work in the morning she wore a long-sleeved shirt and carried an ice-pick in her sleeve.

*****

On her way to work one morning, Lashaun noticed a man who just seemed out of place. She was pretty used to the neighbourhood and was sure he was not from there. She had never seen him in the community before. When she came close to him he moved into her pathway. She was terrified.

"Doops (my friend) you know Lizard?" the man said to Lashaun.

"No." She really didn't know who he was asking for but she wanted to make the conversation as short as possible.

"You know Lizard man, the tall youth, live just down this road." He was adamant.

"Unless he has another name I don't know anybody named Lizard." She wanted to be out of his air. *"Ask somebody else 'cause I'm late for work."*

The man who was almost two feet taller than Lashaun, was now following her. She wanted to run. She imagined him just taking out his 9mm and shooting her in the head. She wanted to get rid of him. As she approached the main road she noticed a taxi passing by.

7

"Taxi!" she yelled, *"town?"*

She began to run towards the taxi but realized the man was also running along. When they reached the taxi, he opened the door for her to get in. She went in thinking he would just close it and go but he was also on his way in. She had to think quickly. She had to come up with a plan. She had to figure a way out of this. She could stab him with the ice-pick and run, but what if she missed, he would probably just kill her.

"Stop driver! I have to get out, forgot something!" she didn't realize she was yelling.

The driver stopped the car and she walked back up the street. The man continued in the taxi. Not wanting to seem suspicious she pretended to walk back. When the car turned the corner, she stopped by the bus stop and waited for a few minutes before she got on the JUTC bus. To stay out of harm's way she took the bus to work instead of the usual 'Halfway Tree route Coaster bus'. Lashaun was frightened for her life. What if he had out smarted her? What if she turned around and he was right there?

*****

When she told Princess the story, Princess thought she was being paranoid. She didn't know the man Lashaun described and sincerely wondered if Lashaun was hallucinating. In the evening when she accompanied Princess to the taxi instead of her usual jogging as she used to, Lashaun sprinted down the street, into the one bed roomed house and locked the door behind her. For the next few weeks on the job she sprinted to grab her taxi. It wasn't too long though that her fears lessened. No-one had directly harmed her, neighbours still said their hellos and continued to beg and borrow from the couple and everything seemed normal.

9

Things didn't stay that way for long. Over a year after the very first threat on the women's lives was made, rumours were now widespread of a contract out for their lives. It was Lashaun who laughed it off this time.

"Mouth make to say anything," She told her girlfriend, *"this is not a movie."*

This time around Princess was much more concerned because she had heard it from her friends in the community. Her friends were known to butt heads with some very notorious characters in the area and had overheard them talking about killing the women.

"Princess find somewhere else to live man 'cause they're serious. They're getting paid and you know a lot of people will do anything for the money. You're making enough money, go, and rent a place up in Red Hills or somewhere else. But run for your life." her friend warned fretfully.

10

Princess was petrified. She knew her friends must have heard something terrible to have given her such a warning. But could she really afford to move and what if they saw them moving out? If they wanted to kill them so badly they would probably do so when they were moving out. It was only when she told Lashaun what Vinette had said that, she also became frightened. She was now back in her old state; scared for her life. She was so afraid that the following morning instead of going to work she stopped at the nearby police station to report the threats being made on her life. She was told there was nothing they could do about it as it was only hear-say. Running out of options she rushed home woke Princess from her sleep and the two began to unpack their clothes from the chest of drawers. They were heading as far away as they could get they told themselves. They made a plan.

*****

Over the next few weeks the two would take a few pieces of their belongings with them each time they left the house to the homes of friends or family. They planned their getaway. They didn't want to be killed while they were moving out so no one could know.

Princess had arranged the move with a friend from the club she worked at. He would pick them up Saturday night, at the time Princess was expected to leave for work. They would take just enough that their regular bags could carry that night and would dress up as though they were heading out for a night on the town. But their plans would soon crumble.

There is a saying in Jamaica "Never let your right hand know what your left hand is doing." The proverb simply means; if you want to keep it a secret do not repeat it. Unfortunately, Princess had told one of her friends about their plan. Jessica meant no harm to the couple but just

12

couldn't keep it to herself and news travels very fast with a population not exceeding three million. Before you knew it, the plan had reached the ears of the wrong people.

*****

The couple tried to appear as 'normal' as possible. Lashaun was now out of a job and so most of her time was spent at home. At about 5:45am Princess had crawled into bed beside her girlfriend. The women slept until about 11am then Lashaun got up and made breakfast. Because most of the couple's clothes were out of the house they were now doing their laundry two or three times per week. After breakfast, the two went outside in the yard they shared with two other families to do their laundry. They completed that task then were back in their one bed roomed house where they spent the rest of the day. Princess cooked dinner, they watched a few movies then Princess was ready for work. The two walked to the taxi, they said their goodbyes then

13

Princess got into a taxi and was off. It was Thursday night, usually there would be quite a number of people in the street but there wasn't many tonight. Lashaun ran home and locked the door behind her.

Having trouble sleeping because of the noise coming from a nearby dance-hall she decided to put on a movie and turned the volume up more than usual. She could still hear the music coming from the nearby sound system but couldn't hear distinct sounds outside because of the sound confusion of the TV and music. She was just about dosing off when she heard banging on the door. She didn't respond. She reached under her bed for her machete. She came down from the bed and tiptoed to stand between the fridge and chest of drawer. When the banging continued she kneeled between the furniture and began to dial her girlfriend, but Princess didn't pick up. Unable to compose herself she laid flat on the floor trying to peep under the door. She recognized a familiar voice calling from outside the door but refused to answer. Not long after, the knocking stopped and so did the calling.

She quietly crawled back to the bed. Thoughts huddled in her head. What if they started shooting through the walls? She kept trying to get Princess on the phone but no response. She wanted to hear if anything was going on in the yard but she was afraid to lower the volume on the TV. If the person was still waiting outside they would know she was awake. When Princess finally rang back she rushed to answer the call but a sudden banging on the window next to her bed made her realize she wasn't yet out of harm's way.

"*Hello babes.*' out of breath from her nocturnal activities Princess awaited her girlfriend's response on the other end. When it didn't come she hung up and rang again thinking she had a bad connection. After one ring Lashaun picked up.

15

"Babes?" there was no response. *"Shaun?'* still no answer.

Lashaun hung up for the second time. Princess rang again and again, each time on the first ring Lashaun picked up. This time, after saying hello twice and not getting a response, Princess knew something was wrong.

"Oh god! Shaun is somebody in the house? Lord have mercy! Hang up I'm gonna call the police! Oh god!"

She hurriedly hung up from Lashaun and immediately phoned the police.

"119 emergency how can I direct your call?"
"Police please!' she screamed into the receiver.
"Ma'am what's your location?"

"Uptown Kingston!" she exclaimed without even thinking, and she was put through to the half way tree police station.

"Halfway Tree police station how may I help you?" an officer answered her call.

"I need the police down South, I need help! There are about 6 or 7 men in my neighbour's yard. She's a little old woman and they are trying to get through the window. Help please!"

"Ma'am you have the wrong police station."

"What? I need THE POLICE! They're going to break in and kill the woman."

"Ma'am you're closer to central so it's better if you call there, they could respond quicker."

"Listen," Princess was becoming agitated, *"I just need the police to come and check it out and you need to send someone now. I am looking out the window now and two of the men are trying to break down the door."*

The officer asked for the address and told Princess she'd get someone to check it out. She called Lashaun back to inform her that the police were on their way. Lashaun whispered to her that it seemed the perpetrators had left but she still wanted the police to stop by. Not even a minute after she hung up with Princess, Lashaun was frightened by loud banging on her window again.

"*Gal open the bloodclaat door!*' a male's voice shouted outside her window. The voice reminded her of the man she had met while on the way to work over a year ago, the man who had asked about Lizard. She didn't know what to do but she was not going to respond. The banging continued for over half an hour and still the police didn't come. The nearest police station was less than 15 minutes away from the house. She rang Princess and said nothing. Their communication was spot on. Princess this time called the central police station herself. She told them of the incident and they were hearing of it for the first time.

When the police finally got there one of the officers had seen men running away from the house. They went into the yard but Lashaun's door was the last for them to knock on. She was still frightened and didn't know if she could trust the officers so she didn't respond to their call either. She was happy they were there but her coming out to them might endanger her life she thought. They would just ask if she was ok inside and then would be off again she rationalised. If the men who were outside her door were watching from close by, they would know for sure that she was inside. She heard the officers move around the yard then drove away.

Lashaun couldn't fall asleep she yearned for day light and for Princess to come home. But in just an hour her worst fears approached. The door was kicked in. She was too shocked to scream. One of the men came over with his gun and slapped her across the face with it.

"What, do you think the police could save you?" the other questioned as he eagerly undressed himself. *"I'm going to show you a real man, Lizard take off her clothes."*

Lashaun kept backing away 'til she was back against the wall. She was hysterical. She held her clothes to her body and pleaded for her life.

"Please I beg you, I have AIDS don't rape me. Please.'

The first man laughed. *"Sodomite have AIDS? Bomboclaat, you take me for an idiot?"*

"Please I'm not a lesbian, please. Oh god!" she was frantic.

The first man grabbed her, flung her to the bed and began to rip her clothes off. She kept crossing her legs and fighting but her physical strength couldn't match his. Soon she was naked on the bed.

"Raas Lizard, look at her figure. Mi raas!" The second man exclaimed.

Lashaun reached for the ice-pick below her pillow while the men laughed amongst themselves. Taking it into her grip she placed her hand beneath her, attempting to derive a plan. She would wait until he came atop her then would stab him in the back and run out of the house. She wasn't sure it would work but she would take her chances. When the two fixated their gaze on her again Lashaun kept wailing.

"Oh God, please just let me go, please. I won't tell anybody please." She begged them.

"Gal, shut up!" the first man said.

When the man came atop her she recognized him from the street; the man asking for Lizard. As he tried to penetrate her she swung her hand from beneath her but just before

21

the ice-pick reached his skin, the onlooker grabbed her hand. He wrestled the tool from her and they both began to beat her. When they ceased the beating Lizard sat behind her, bounded her hands with his and hugged her with his thighs. The other man tied her legs wide part to the legs of the bed. First, he used the ice-pick to rape her over and over again. With her mouth bounded Lashaun made no sounds. She thought it would please them more if she cried and though it was unbearable she made no sounds. He soon began to finger her vagina.

"Jah know star, the gal pussy good." He told his friend while he continued to ravage her body. Still she did not cry.

When the first was finished raping her the second began his course. This time he forced her to perform oral sex on him. She bit him on his penis and he butted her with his gun over the head. Blood streamed down her face but Lashaun did not cry or scream. She just laid there. He

22

untied her legs and threw her on her stomach and sodomized her. He ejaculated inside her, picked her up by the hair and whispered.

"I guess now you're double positive. I just gave you another dose of AIDS."

With all the strength she could sum-up Lashaun bellowed out for God's help.

The man who had first raped her turned her over again on her back and while he forced his arm inside her vagina and the tissues ripped, he said *"I work for the police and I have eyes everywhere,"* then he giggled, *"you're done now, you never had any use for your pussy anyway."*

The men dressed and told her they weren't killing her because she was already dead. *"You can hang yourself now."* Lizard said before he left the house.

She couldn't move from where they had left her. She was ashamed to call out for help. Naked on the bed and covered in blood she just laid there. Not crying, not thinking, just lying there.

*****

Princess came home about an hour after the men had left the house. She couldn't finish her shift, she knew something was terribly wrong. She felt it. When she got into the house she was weakened to see Lashaun in the state she was. But her instinct kicked into first gear. She raced to wake the only male who was living in the yard. He came to the couple's one-bedroom house and helped Princess carry a motionless Lashaun to the public hospital. When they rushed into the Emergency unit, the nurses were quick to assist.

The police came to question her but Lashaun wouldn't say who raped her. To her, she was already dead, and she didn't want to further endanger Princess. She didn't want her to go through what she had been through. She would suffer and there would be no justice but she couldn't even trust the police. Whether it was true or not, there was a possibility that one of the men who raped her was a police officer.

Princess was there to support her. She kept up with her clinic appointments and three months after her rape Lashaun tested HIV positive.

∧∧∧∧∧

Kizzy

I often sit and think to myself that I can only imagine that my story isn't much different from that of any other woman who had been raped or sexually abused. Most women will tell you that this was done to them by people they know, people they love and thought loved them. Unfortunately, for too many of us this was done by our fathers. And yes, unfortunately, it's not a myth that mothers don't believe when daughters tell them. One would possibly find it hard to believe that mothers would sanction this or even accept it. When I think back I really wish the outcome for me would have been different but at the end of the day we are where we are in life at any given moment.

I didn't even know I was a lesbian until all of this happened and it all happened way too fast. I didn't get the opportunity to take things in slowly, mull them over and then make decisions; my world literally became a whirlwind in less than a day.

*****

My father came home from work and I was outside playing in the yard with my neighbour Irene. Strangely, we have remained the best of friends over the years and though sometimes even the thought of her brings back some of the most painful memories, she also remains the most constant part of my life. Irene and I were playing house. We were the only kids on our street of the same age group, all the other kids were either too young or too old. She was 13 and I was 12. He seemed angry, my father. He chased Irene away and demanded that I come into the house.

I was too confused to negotiate with him, so I ran into the house crying. I was confused because my father was not usually like this. He was not a confrontational man. He'd never as much as gotten angry with me or spoken loudly. Before that day he was my hero, my absolute all. He was kind and caring.

We lived in a three-bedroom house. After being shouted at by my father I headed straight to my room and locked myself in weeping from plain embarrassment and fright. My mother was not home. She had left moments before my father had arrived home. She had a bible study with the ladies from church. I wanted her to be home to soothe my pain.

My parents and I attended the Pentecostal church two streets from us. They were devoted Christians, and I too believed in the church. Only weeks after my 12th birthday I had been baptised. We believed in committing our lives to Christ and living according to the teachings of the bible. We never missed church on Sundays and

28

attended bible study during the week too. Often times, we would have someone staying over in our house who was in need. This, my mother said, is what God would expect us to do; help others.

I heard my father knock on the door but it was as though he was trying to beat down the door. It scared me. The door didn't have a lock so it was only closed but he didn't come in. He kept beating on the door, so I got up to open it.

"God doesn't like ugly!" he screamed. *"You will go to hell for your sins! Hell!"*

His eyes seemed dark. It was as though he was possessed. He scared me. I wasn't sure what he was angry about. He pushed his way into my room and proceeded to drag me with him.

29

"It's un-natural! Girls are supposed to like boys, not other girls!"

"Daddy what do you mean?" I was confused. He seemed to be filled with rage.

He responded by demanding that I take my clothes off. I became filled with terror as I saw him unbuckle his belt. Though my father had never beaten me, I assumed that's what he was going to do. Boy was I wrong.

When he was finished and my sheets were soaked with blood, I had still been crying when he demanded that I go bathe myself. I was in the shower unable to wash myself, confused, sore and hurt when my father came in.

"You are a child of God! A child of God! Over my dead body will you turn into one of them. By the grace of God."

I kept sobbing. I suppose he realised I couldn't or wouldn't bathe myself so he bathed me. In my room, my bed had been cleared and new sheets had been put on. A new set of clothes were laid out on the bed for me. My father creamed my skin and dressed me. All this time I couldn't stop sobbing and the sight of him made me sick and confused yet at the same time I was in pain and wanted my father to hold me and make it better. I wanted my mother to come home. I wanted God to take away the pain. I wanted to wake up from the dream. But it wasn't a dream, it wasn't going away.

*****

My mother returned home after what seemed like years later. I was weak, I wanted to run into her arms but I couldn't. She came to me on the couch where I had been crying.

"*Kizzy, what's wrong pumpkin?*" She asked frantically. When I didn't respond she searched my body for bruises.

"*She wasn't looking in the right place.*" I thought.

"*Fred!*" she screamed, "*what's wrong with Kizzy? What's wrong with my child?*"

"*She's alright now, she's fixed*" my father said, as he walked into the room sobbing.

My mother fell back on the floor screaming "*No! No! No! Jesus no!*"

My father cradled my mother as she wept. I was lost. They both seemed to know something I didn't. My father had hurt me and I was in pain but it was my mother and father who comforted each other. I was the one who was hurting, I was the one who had been hurt.

*****

The following day before school my parents came to pray with me. It was then that I had finally realised what had happened. My mother prayed that God would take away my feelings and make me natural. She prayed that I would be fixed and explicitly asked God that he would help me realise that the feelings I had for Irene, the way I was with her, was a sin. She prayed for my father and that God would reward him for saving his child and keeping his house in order.

My mother told me that what my father did was for my own good and that he had fixed me. She told me that I wasn't allowed to tell anyone else about it and made me promise I wouldn't. I promised.

*****

That day changed my life. I could never look at my parents the same again. How could the two people I loved the most in the world hurt me so bad and how could God allow this when he himself claimed to love me? I wanted to be rid of them.

I ran away when I was 14 for the first time and after a few times I was put into a girl's home. I was finally rid of them. I've been through a lot in the system but I was better off. I hated my parents. Some days I think I still do. We don't have a relationship and I don't want one with them. I doubt they would want one with me either. So, in essence we are all better off.

I am a lesbian woman and I have had to learn the hard way over the years that this is okay and this is who I am. In my opinion, it is a natural part of me. How can I think any different when even the people who brought me into this world knew it long before I knew it myself?

^^^^^

Ms. Mavis

I've taken three buses to get here and now I have been walking on this road for the last 28 minutes to be exact. Finally, I can see her at the top of the hill. From here she looks so frail, I want to tell her to sit and wait for me to get there. I'm worried she'll fall. I'm intrigued by her for a number of reasons and one is her age. She's an 86-years-old woman who's lived through so many different "times". I see her as a wealth of knowledge and wisdom. Sadly though, I am here to learn about what happened to her years ago. I'm here to take account of her rape.

She's stronger than she looked from the bottom of the hill.

"What happen baby? Glad to see that you reach safe." She said in the most hospitable Jamaican way reaching out to hug me.

It is a warm hug, one that makes you feel as though you have come home to a better place.

She's taken out the good china. Cornmeal pudding is on the fire still, and the pumpkin soup is ready to be plated. I'm worried about her moving around so much but she assures me that she's stronger than she looks and can manage just fine.

"Those days when Mary was alive she always wanted me to settle down just the same, but I always tell her that one day I will rest. I have breath and strength so I give God thanks and carry on." She seems to be talking to herself now when she said, *"I miss her though, it's lonely now."*

"Who is Mary?" I questioned unsure whether it was okay to ask.

"Oh child, she was the love of my life. You know we were together for 42 years before she went home? The doctors down by the hospital say they couldn't help her because the cancer was too far gone." She paused. Sighed, then continued. *"She had a good life, we had a lot of good times together, you know?"*

"Sorry to hear, Ms. Mavis." I felt bad now for asking.

"No, no, she's happy now my child, no more pain. She had it rough in the last few days. So even though I miss her I'm happy she went home." She handed me a big bowl of soup. *"You must eat."*

I smiled accepting the bowl of soup I know will take me a long time to finish but know that even if it kills me I must finish it.

*****

Ms. Mavis tells me of her life in a time that I only know about through my great grandparents and the older people I surround myself with. She tells me of how she

37

walked miles and miles to get to different places and how she has experienced the changes over the years.

She had gotten married when she was only 18 to a boy just up the street from where she lived. The marriage was a family decision and according to her it was 'good for the family'. Her parents were well off and when she matured and it was time to take a husband it was important for them that she married someone of the same stature or better. Thomas was also from a good family and was well off. Mavis had no attraction to him and had never spent time with him but she had to get married and Thomas was the one.

Once married, they started living together in the house bought by their parents also within the neighbourhood they grew up. Thomas became a doctor and Mavis became a teacher of English and Literature at the top high school in their parish where she taught for over 35 years. Mavis recalls a life with Tom with almost no sex. She said he was kind and understanding and like her knew something was amiss. They loved each other and in her opinion, he was a good man but she never felt the way she thought that a woman should feel about the man she was meant to spend the rest of her life with.

In 1951 Tom fell in-love with a girl from the hospital and he and Mavis divorced the same year.

"I was happy for him. He came home so excited and sad at the same time to tell me about her but I understood and I wanted that for him." Mavis said with contentment on her face.

*****

In the summer of 1959, Mavis met Mary and fell madly in love.

"I remember it like it was yesterday. She was wearing a pleated knee length dress with round collar and she wore this wide brimmed hat, unlike any I had seen before. She was so poised. The sun danced on her skin. Our eyes met, more like she caught me staring at her from across the street," a very innocent giggle escaped Mavis. *"She was beautiful, Mary; very pretty. Her eyes lit up and my knees buckled when she walked up to me. From that day on we were together until her very last breath."*

Mavis seemed to have escaped to another world then finally she said, *"You know, I had a good life with my Mary. We were so in-love. In all our years, we never once had an argument, not once. We were like two perfectly matched peas in a pod."* She wonders off again.

Mary was seven years Mavis' senior and was a widow with a son who was 21 at the time they met. Her son was troubled she said and was still living at home with her. For over a year Mary and Mavis had their rendezvous at Mavis' home where they soon began to spend most of their time. Mary also a teacher, soon got a job at the same school Mavis taught at and the two were inseparable.

After being together for almost two years Mary introduced her son David to Mavis. David was very angry with his mother for bringing the two of them together.

"I remember the boy saying, "I don't want to be mixed up in this nastiness". He was so angry with his mother and he really went off the handle. I didn't know what to do but I didn't want Mary staying in that house with him so I kindly told him we were leaving and I took her away back to my house. It broke her heart. I could tell. She never spoke much about it but I knew that it really hurt her to hear him speak the way he did and discard her. They stopped speaking and she stopped going to the house."

*****

Mavis recalls her dogs barking hysterically in the early morning while she was busy preparing Mary's bath. She recalls the two of them huddled together trying to look out the kitchen window to see what was going on. But before they knew it David was screaming inside the house behind them.

"When I saw him, I wasn't scared at all. In my mind, the boy was upset and would just maybe tell us where to get off and leave. But when his mother walked towards him I saw his eyes literally turn over. It was as though I was faced by the devil himself. No amount of talking could calm the boy down." she tells me.

Filled with rage David attacked his mother knocking her to the floor. When Mavis, raced to help Mary, he attacked her too.

"You know, that was the worse day of my life. I tried not to hold on to it but I do remember it very well. And for Mary's sake I forgave him. I know it was painful for her to watch and it ruined their relationship. She never spoke to the boy from that day. She wanted nothing to do with him."

Tears came flowing down her cheeks and her voice became shaky. I became overwhelmed with deep sadness for her.

"For years Mary, would awake in the night screaming "come off her, come off her". She said it was the same dream of the boy on top of me, me just lying there on the floor not moving." Mavis was sobbing now. *"I didn't fight him. I didn't want him to turn on Mary. When the boy was finally done, he spat at me and then urinated all over me on the floor. I didn't give him the satisfaction of reacting."*

Mavis recalls staying off work for almost the entire term. She struggled with anxiety after the incident and no matter how much she had convinced herself that no one at school would hurt her she couldn't bring herself to get out of the house let alone go to school.

"The worst part in all of this is what it did to Mary. She never spoke to the boy again and I could tell it tore her up inside. No mother wants to be separated from their child." Mavis said with a distant look in her eyes. *"Before she died he turned up at the house and he apologised to me but Mary still didn't say a word to the boy. Even at her funeral he was still apologising."*

After a few minutes of silence, Mavis spoke *"the problem is baby, no amount of sorry can fix these things. And to make matters worse there are still too many people who would do the exact same thing. They still think that a woman MUST be with a man. We are their property you know. That's what they think; men and women alike."*

∧∧∧∧∧

Tracey

The greatest lesson I have learned in the last few months is that in order to forgive others I must first forgive myself. It has taken me a long time to learn this and in the process, I have ended up hurting myself more than they had.

When my girlfriend's HIV+ uncle, Chris, told me that he would rape me because I had corrupted his niece I had looked at it just as something said in anger. In my mind, the comment/threat had died with the argument. As time passed we all got to a point where we were cordial with each other. I was invited to different family events and though no one acknowledged me as her partner, they weren't very aggressive about the situation either. It was more that they all knew we were in a relationship but didn't talk about it. At least not around us.

45

We were together for almost five years before I moved in with her in the same yard where her mother and two uncles lived with their families. We stayed in a two-bedroom house we were renting from the same landlord as all the others. Things were pretty "normal", we seemed like the perfect extended family. I even believed we were. There were times we had our disagreements but all in all we all got along.

*****

Tamara next door, had a child who was eight years old and rumoured to be the child of Chris. He never accepted the child but I quite liked him and Tamara, and often helped out with whatever I could; she was a struggling single parent.

I was sitting on the veranda on a Thursday afternoon on my day off from work when Tamara came by to see me.

"What's up Trace?" She'd asked.

"Nothing much, just trying to catch the breeze. You ok?"

"Yes man, everything's ok. Can you come over and help me with this really quick?"

With no hesitation, I followed her. *"What do you need help with?"* She didn't respond. When we entered her house, she closed the door behind us. This wasn't like her.

"I want to talk to you about something, but you can't repeat it to anyone." She seemed frightened, looking around the room and through the window as if she was making sure we were entirely alone. *"I really like you and I know you're a good person so I'm telling you but please remember I have a child Tracey. You can't say this to anyone."*

"Tamara, what's wrong? Just say it! You're scaring the hell out of me now," I demanded.

47

"You need to promise me you won't get me into trouble for this. I'm only looking out for you as a woman. Promise me."

"Okay, okay, I promise! Just tell me please." My heart was pounding now.

"They are planning to do something to you. I don't know if it's you and Shan or just you but you need to go where they can't find you. You have....."

"What do you mean? Do what? Who?" I interrupted.

"Chris and them. I don't know who else is involved but I heard him talking to someone and they were planning."

"Planning what?"

"Tracey, they don't like that you and Shan are together. Her mother is the main one and they want to get rid of you. I don't know what they are planning but I know that it's violent because they are planning to take you."

"But you said you weren't sure. Are they going to do something to Shan?" I wasn't sure whether to believe her. She had no reason to lie but why now? I'd been around for years and I've always spent a lot of time around them. If

they wanted to hurt me or Shan there were more than enough opportunities in the past for them to do it.

"I don't know. I honestly don't know, but that family would never do anything to hurt their own. You on the other hand are not one of them."

She was right about that. They had a strong bond. They stood up for each other no matter what. If they had a big disagreement or even a physical fight they would be cool with each other again before the day's end. No matter how serious the argument was or how much they had hurt each other, moments later it would seem as though nothing had happened between them.

"Wow," I sighed, *"I don't even know what to think now."*

"Tracey, please you're a young beautiful girl with your whole life ahead of you. Just call it a loss and run for your life. They are notorious and it will be just you against them."

49

"I need to call my brother." All I could think of was that I needed to feel safe.

"Where's your phone?"

"I didn't bring it. But wait, I need to talk with Shan. I need to call her."

"Shan's number is in my phone." She was handing her phone to me but she paused. *"Wait, wait, wait is that even a good idea? What if she knows what's going on? Then you call from my phone and I will be caught up in it as well."*

Shan wouldn't do anything to hurt me, I thought. We love each other. Whatever they are planning, if they are planning anything for that matter, Shan doesn't know about it.

"Do you want me to go get your phone?"

"No, it's ok. I'll get it."

"You need to wipe your eyes though because they will know something is going on if you go back looking like that."

"No one is there, everyone is at work or school."

"Okay." she said.

I walked back to the house, Tamara trailed behind me.

For some reason, I couldn't bring myself to calling my brother. I wasn't sure what I would say or what he would say or do. I wasn't sure that what I was hearing was the truth. I couldn't understand why Chris or anyone else here would want to hurt me. And if it was the truth, what were they planning to do to me? What would happen if I told my brother, would he also be thinking the way I'm thinking?

Tamara stood at the side of the house now, as though she was watching out for someone. All this time she was sweating profusely seeming very anxious and terrified.

"It's almost time for me to go collect Gregory at school. Please don't tell anyone what I've said, I'm begging you."

51

"Don't worry about it, I won't say anything."

*****

For the next few days I felt as though I was living in a different world. I couldn't function at work. I just didn't know what to think or what to expect. I wasn't eating either.

"Baby what's going on with you?" Shan had asked one evening while we were having dinner.

"Nothing, I'm okay."

"No but you're not yourself."

"I'm okay, for real." I tried to force a smile.

"Okay but why haven't you been eating. It's not just today either, you've been like this for days." she paused. *"Are you upset with me? Did I do something wrong?"*

"No Shan, I'm okay." The last few days I had been reserved and somewhat unsure of who I could trust at this point. I was even questioning her loyalty.

"Okay then, if you say you're alright then I guess that you are."

*****

Shan was on the night shift and for some reason I had completely forgotten until she started getting dressed close to 9pm. Her shift was a 10 to 7. As she was getting ready for work I felt a grave level of fear and uneasiness come over me.

"I don't think I want to stay here tonight."

"What do you mean? Where do you want to go?"

"I don't know, It's a bit late but maybe I can stay with Grace until tomorrow. I should give her a call."

"*Tracey, what's the problem? Why do you all of a sudden want to sleep out? Has something happened?*" She had now knelt in front of the bed between my knees.

"*Baby, I just don't want to be here alone. I don't feel right.*" I was sobbing now.

She held me, "*Sorry baby, do you want me to call in sick?*"

"*Let me call Grace and see if I can stay there.*" I rang Grace but she was away in Negril with her girlfriend.

"*I'm going to call in sick, I can't leave you like this.*"

"*No don't do that, just go.*"

"*Okay then, do you want to stay with Mommy?*"

"*If she's okay with that, yes.*"

She rang her mother who said I could spend the night on her couch. I didn't feel comfortable but I didn't want her to take the night off all because I was 'feeling uncomfortable'. For all I know, I was feeling uneasy because I completely forgot she was on the night shift. I would go stay with her mother.

I was more uneasy at her mother's than I was at our place so I came back home just after 11pm, had a shower and got into bed. After tossing and turning for what seemed like days, I finally fell asleep.

In the middle of the night I was frightened by movements in the house. It was dark. The lights were off and the curtains blocked out whatever little light the moon, stars, or nearby street lights could have provided. I couldn't see who was there and they tried to be very quiet but I could hear them breathe.

"Who's that?"

No one answered. I sat up in bed wanting to turn the lights on but instead of touching the bedside lamp next to the bed I touched someone's leg.

"Awwwwwwwwwwwwwwwwwwwww!!!!!" I screamed. Then someone covered my mouth.

"Put the light on quick." a voice said.

In what seemed like seconds the lights came on and there were three men and Chris in the room.

"No please, please Chris." I begged without knowing what they were there to do to me.

"Don't call my name!" he growled.

"Bring her." the man at the bedroom door said.

"Jesus Christ! Please Chris!" I screamed. But the guy who had covered my mouth earlier did the same thing again. He threw me over his shoulder now and walked me to the living room. I was still screaming but no one was coming to my rescue.

"Chris!!! Pleaseeeeeeeee!!! Oh God please NO!!!"""

"Gal shut up!" he booted me. *"Just hurry up with this."* Chris told his companions.

My head was spinning now. I felt as though my head was swaying from side to side and growing at the same time. I made up my mind to scream for my life. *"Dawn!!!! Help me."* I screamed at the top of my lungs.

I got up to run and was shoved back to the couch. Someone was now pinning me down.

"Just take off her clothes," one of the men said.

I knew now what they were there to do but I wasn't sure how far they were going to take it. The only thing going through my mind at this point was that Chris couldn't rape me. He was HIV positive. Even if they did not kill me there and then it would be as though they did. I kept thinking that I have to fight for my life. I started to scream again.

I wasn't sure whether time had stopped or that Dawn just didn't care. She was right next door in a three-bedroom attached to ours. On any given day, she could hear the TV from our living room and ask me to turn down the volume. She wasn't a sound sleeper either. Why wasn't she coming to my rescue?

Why didn't I run when Tamara told me to? I wonder if she can hear me? Will she come to help me? She wouldn't be able to fight them off anyway.

I was kicking and pushing the man off me. Soon another came to pin my hands down. The man who had ordered them to take me into the living room was now unbuttoning his pants. He slowly walked over to me on the couch. Chris and one of the men pulling my legs apart, the other still pinning my hands down. I wasn't going to make it easy for them. I kicked with all my might and screamed with every bit of strength I could muster. But the man forced himself inside me.

"Stop now, stop." Dawn appeared in the living room. I couldn't believe what I was hearing. It was as though she was ordering her employees. The man continued as though he had not heard her speak. *"Stop now!"* she exclaimed. *"The police are coming."* She was now walking over to me arms folded over her bosom. She picked up my panties from the floor and threw them at me. *"Tomorrow you need to find somewhere to go and leave my daughter alone! And believe me not even the entire police force can save you if I see you after tomorrow,"* her voice riddled with scorn and resentment.

I didn't feel afraid anymore. I had already heard her say that the police were coming so I was anticipating their arrival. The men left and I ran out into the street to meet the police but they weren't there yet. I ran to wake Tamara. *"Tamara, open the door!"* the lights did not come on and the door did not open. I kept banging down the door. But she never came.

I soon heard the sirens very close so I ran back to the street and they were already there. Dawn was standing by the gate to our yard speaking to one of the officers. I ran towards them.

"Help me please, they raped me!" I was shaking the policeman.

"Lady calm down" the policeman said.

"Nobody raped her," Dawn said, *"I caught her in the house with a man, now she's claiming she was raped."*

"What's wrong with her face? Her face is swollen," said the other officer.

60

"Well officer you can charge me for that. I was angry so I kicked her."

"That's not what happened!!!!" I shrieked. *"I've been raped!"*

After what seemed like hours of "he said she said", Dawn not copping to anything and the police not finding anyone in the yard or in Chris' house; the police took me to the hospital.

*****

No one was charged with anything. Shan didn't seem to believe anything I was saying either. After days of trying to get them to admit it and trying to get the police to look for the men I described to them I decided to leave it alone. I walked away from my relationship with her too. It wasn't so much because of what her family did. It was the fact that she didn't believe me.

Unfortunately, I have for many years let it define my life and hold me back in a lot of ways. Trust seemed impossible for a very long time and for years I didn't date anyone. I barely went out with friends or made efforts to maintain my friendships. Trust is still a big struggle.

I've not been with anyone intimately since. I have learned to forgive myself, because for a long time I took all the blame. I kept thinking that I should have left when Tamara told me, that I shouldn't have moved there because Chris had once threatened to rape me. I just kept blaming myself for all of it. But I've learned to let go. I've learned that it wasn't my fault and that I wasn't responsible for their actions or lack of it.

Like my therapist says, *"It was a bad thing that happened to me but it's not who I am"*

^^^^^

Alex

"What's that?!" she fell back on the floor, startled.

"What are you talking about?" I knew exactly what she meant.

"There's something between your legs!"

"No there isn't." All the passion we had walking in the door a moment ago had now been sucked out of the air. I walked over to the refrigerator, opened the door and got a beer. *"Do you want something to drink?"*

"Are we not going to talk about this?"

"We don't need to. I'm good."

"But..."

"But nothing. Let's not do this now!" I was impatient. I didn't want to talk about it. *"Are you going home or sleeping here?"*

"Don't talk to me like that." She was now gathering her stuff. *"Where's my blouse?"*

"Come here."

"Don't touch me!"

"I'm sorry, come here. You know you want to."

"No, I don't." She was trying to hide her smile now. *"You don't talk to me about anything. You are always keeping me at a distance. Do you think anyone would believe that we have been seeing each other for almost eight months and I've never even seen you naked? Like what's all that about? It's as though you don't trust me. So, what's the point then?"*

"Calm down." I stood up to cradle her.

I had long fallen for her but just like the ones before her I knew it wouldn't go anywhere. Eventually she will have had enough and would move on. It wasn't that I didn't want to be open with her, I just couldn't be. I didn't know how to trust anyone anymore.

"I'm sorry." I told her.

*****

I've been having the same nightmare since it happened. In the dream, I'm screaming for my mother, but she never comes. When I finally get up from under him I can see the blood flowing down my inner thighs. Each time I awake covered in sweat; feeling as though I had been running a marathon. I fail to fall asleep after. Lying awake each time, I feel the tears flow down my temples and into my ears. I don't feel any form of emotion yet the tears flow. My mind is blank as I stare into the darkness. Every time it's the same; awoken from the nightmare, lying there unable to fall asleep again.

What Kerry felt between my thighs was the scar. The physical reminder of what happened to me. There was no escaping this. It was something I had to face every day

65

sometimes too often. I hated showering, each time unable to avoid it. But, on the days when I was emotionally torn I kept trying to wash it away; spending hours in the shower. It's an irrational state. It can't be washed away.

*****

"How much further do we have to go?" I asked.

"Just a little further. We are almost there."

"You said that a while back and we are still driving. Couldn't they meet us half way?"

"We are almost there. Turn Left."

She hissed, *"we've been driving for long now Theresa. Are you sure you know where we are going?"*

"I've been here loads of times before, we are almost there."

"Ok ma'am."

"On a serious note though they need to move from this bush-up place. And now I really need to use the bathroom."

"We are almost there right? So, you can use theirs?"

"Wait pull over, I don't think I can hold it."

"We can't stop here. It's too dark. I don't think it's safe. How much further do we have to go?"

"Alex, just pull over. I can't hold it. Otherwise I might just go on the seat!" She was doing the pee dance now. *"pull over please."*

"Really? I prefer if you wet the seat. It's too dark and lonely here. No one in sight."

"Turn right, turn right!!"

I almost missed the turn. *"Pay attention! That was dangerous. How much further are we really going Theresa?"*

"Okay, not far now. Just one more turn then we are there."

"Yes, one more turn, but how far?"

POW! The tyre blew and the car swerved, I hurriedly slammed on the brakes. Luckily, I'd not been going fast and the road was rocky.

"Lex!"

"Fuck! Now this."

"I have to pee," she sprung from the car and went to urinate on the side of the road.

"There's someone coming up the road, hurry up."

"Okay, okay, almost done."

The human frame in the distance had now turned off the road we were on up ahead. I wanted to go after the person to get some help but Theresa was still not done and I didn't want to leave her alone.

"I thought you said someone was coming," she was standing next to me.

"Yeah but the person turned. Why is it so lonely up here? Can we walk to where they live?"

"I think we can but do you think it's safe to leave the car alone?"

"We can come get it later. Don't worry. We need a flashlight so I can change the tyre and I hope they have one because I do not intend to stay here tonight."

"I'm sure we can get help, come."

"Take your handbag so I can lock the car."

It was dark and lonely. So much different from the city. It was just after 10 at night and it seemed the entire neighbourhood was on lock down. I found it strange. Other than the person I had seen earlier there was no one out. No cars on the road either. I could tell Theresa was afraid though she didn't say. Her grip was so firm on my arm everything below my elbow was numb after only walking up the road for a few minutes.

"Wait, do you see that?"

"Yes, I think so. It's people, right? Do you want to go over there though?"

"I don't know. Maybe not. We are almost at their house anyway. See where the light is in that window? That's where they live."

"Yes, let's just continue then."

Soon a voice called out to us. *"Oiy, what's happening? Hold up."*

"Don't stop," I whispered to Theresa, *"let's keep going."*

"Oiy!" He called out again.

"Don't panic," I told her, "don't let him think that we are afraid."

He was next to us now, "everything good?"

"Yeah man, you?"

"Oh, you're a girl. So why are you dressed like that?"

"Like what?"

"Like a man."

Theresa was gripping me tighter now.

"So, what are you doing this side? You ladies definitely aren't from around here. I know every face in this community. Hold on, is this your girl or what? Why's she holding you like that?"

"Why do you ask so many questions?" Theresa questioned impatiently.

"Why are you so jumpy?"

71

She started walking faster, *"just leave us alone!"*

"Sodomite gal, don't talk to me like that!" He hurried towards us.

"Brother, just chill. We don't want any trouble."

"Don't talk to me! Shut up!"

I knew now that we were in trouble. We could run towards the house but, could we both make it?

"Come on, let's go." Theresa tugged my arm and tried walking away, but the man pushed me, I almost lost my balance. I pushed back. I soon realised this was a mistake. He swung at me and I ducked but he'd hit Theresa who just stumbled to the ground.

"We don't want any trouble." I bent over Theresa trying to soothe her pain. Standing over us he looked like a giant; an angry one.

He kicked me in the back of my head and I fell on top of Theresa. I must have gone unconscious. I heard her gagging and turned to see his hands around her neck choking her. He was on top of her.

"*Get off her,*" I felt groggy. I couldn't move. "*Don't.....*"

"*Shut up before you get it too, you fucking bitch!*"

"*Get off her,*" I felt weak. I started crawling over to her. "*Get off!*"

He stood up and almost tripped over his pants dangling around his ankles. He caught himself. He bent over to brandish a very long knife. I tried to crawl away from him but I couldn't find the strength. I felt as though I was going in and out of consciousness.

"Stay away from me," I wasn't sure if he could hear me, I couldn't hear myself.

He was pulling my pants down and I wanted to kick him but my legs wouldn't kick. I tried to get up but I couldn't. Finally, I kicked real hard and he fell back but I still couldn't get up and he was on top of me again.

"Why are you doing this?"

"Shut up!" he started choking me, then penetrated me. *"Shut up!"*

I tried fighting him. I managed to bite into his arm and he pulled off and out of me. I could taste blood. I began to pull away feeling stones being dragged under me.

The last thing I remember was him gripping me by my ears and knocking my head to the ground repeatedly. When I came to, I was in a house I wasn't familiar with and a woman I'd never met before was binding my upper thigh with what seemed like a belt.

"Theresa, where's Theresa?" I'd asked faintly.

"She's awake," the woman said to a man who was on the house phone in the opposite corner of the room. *"Who is Theresa?"* she asked.

I tried to get up but couldn't, *"we were together, the man…"*

"You came here alone dear."

"No no no no," I protested, *"she was with me."*

"Okay, dear. William, leave the phone because no one is answering anyway. Take a walk and see if there's another one outside. She seems sure this Theresa person was with her."

"I'll search outside."

"She's on the road. I left her there. She's on the road."

*****

Theresa couldn't get past any of it. She attempted suicide a few times and eventually succeeded. I came home to find her lying lifeless on our kitchen floor. She left a note to say she couldn't wake up feeling the way she did every day for the rest of her life and I knew exactly what she meant. I couldn't be there for her as much as she needed me to because I didn't have the strength to even get myself through the days.

It is a constant struggle every single day and the scars are a constant reminder. The cut Kerry felt, made it even more impossible, and the nightmares didn't help, it healed with a huge ridged lump. In the back of my head there's a spot where hair no longer grows too.

The rape didn't just hurt me physically and it does not just continue to tear me apart emotionally every single day; it took the life of the woman I thought I was going to spend the rest of my life with. It took everything from me. I visit her mother on weekends to look after her needs and that brings me more pain than anyone can even begin to imagine. She's the image of her so it pains my soul to look at her, but I have to keep coming, because he took her only child and it killed her too. To make matters worse nothing came of it. No one was ever arrested for it, as a matter of fact, it was never pursued. As always, the police couldn't have cared less because who were we but two lesbians who pretty much got what we deserved.

^^^^^

Renae

The day Renae was born was the happiest day of my life. I didn't want to have a baby, I didn't think I was ready. I was only 16 and I got pregnant the very first time I had sex. My mother kicked me out because I didn't want to have an abortion and it was hard. I struggled a lot along the way going to bed many nights without food in my belly to make sure she was fed and cared for. There was nothing I wouldn't do for her. She was a part of me, my everything. All we had was each other. The boy I had sex with was young and refused to step up to the plate and help me with her so it was us against the world. I promised myself and her, that I would never turn my back on my kid no matter what.

As a child she would always complain if I dressed her up in a dress or skirt. Then, after multiple tries and fuss,

I decided to stop torturing her and started dressing her in only shorts and jeans; as she wanted. She was always a tomboy and I wasn't at all surprised when she "came out". I was frightened and offended that she thought that I would reject her but I wasn't surprised. A mother knows and I knew. As a mother in Jamaica when your child comes out to you or even just having a child who is homosexual you live in constant fear; so more than anything else I was afraid for her. You never stop worrying. You pray with all your might for their safety, that somehow before anyone hurts them God would stop them in their tracks. Worrying about her safety was my main concern and I didn't want her to move out or be where I couldn't watch out for her.

*****

When Renae didn't call or come home that night I knew something was wrong. It's a feeling you get in the pit of your stomach. Any mother will tell you that you

79

know when your child is hurting or in trouble. You always know. I went to three different police stations that night trying to get them to help me look for her but no one would give me the time of day. I wasn't a rich mother from Stoney Hill looking for help. I couldn't give them anything in return. They said my child was out partying, that I should go home and sleep. I told them there was no way she wouldn't let me know if she was going to be late in coming home but they didn't take my word for it. Whether, telling them that she was a lesbian was a factor in them refusing to take me seriously I don't know.

I looked everywhere I thought she could be, called all her friends but I couldn't find her and no one had seen her since she left work. I knew that something was wrong. She needed me and I couldn't find her.

"Have you seen or heard from Renae?" No one had the answers.

After 3am I decided to come back home just in case she had shown up. But she wasn't there. I didn't know what to do. I didn't want to call my sister to worry her. I kept telling myself my child would show up. She would show up with some crazy story but she would show up. But no matter how much I tried to convince myself of this I knew something was wrong with her, wherever she was.

*****

Finally, just after 5am my phone rang. I was wide awake sitting by the window waiting helplessly for her to come home.

"Renae! Where are you?"

"Mommy?" her weak voice on the other end called out.

"Mommy is here baby, where are you. Tell me where you are Reanae?"

81

"Mommy I'm d...."

"Baby, just tell me where you are I'll find you."

I could tell that she was injured. She wasn't making sense and I was struggling to hear her because of how faint her voice was.

"Mommy the dump."

I often say that this was just a miracle of God, but immediately it clicked and I knew exactly where she was. I couldn't be wrong, I had to get to her in time. I didn't know how seriously hurt she was.

After ravaging her body and beating her to a pulp they had left her like trash, naked in the dump at Riverton City. It took me and the few men I found out there, searching through the rubbles themselves, to find her.

*****

She always got hassled for the way she dressed, mostly by women, so many of them mothers. We moved a lot, never stayed long in a neighbourhood because as soon as they started I would move away to protect her. I didn't want her to be threatened and made to feel less human. It was my duty to protect her and I was going to do that no matter what.

Renae didn't tell me about the fact that she was being hassled while coming home from work by men standing around on the street corner. I foolishly thought that things were okay. She said they promised to take her and make her a woman! So, they took her when she was on her way home from work that day.

What happened to my daughter was vicious, cruel, just inhumane. Unfortunately, women and girls get raped everyday but the worse part of it is that these men get away with it. The viciousness that Renae was faced with was over and above what anyone could expect and all because she's a lesbian; all because she dressed and acted differently.

I have to live with this every single day and it's pain you can't begin to understand, no true mother wants to know that they couldn't protect their child. I couldn't protect her that night and I can't save her from what she's going through. I watch her crumble and break day in day out; trying to put things back together but unable to.

*****

Renae wants to forget about this and I don't blame her. I wish I could take it all back; that I could fix it, that it hadn't happened.

I'm sharing this because I want to achieve two things. Firstly, I want mothers to know that their children are their children and they need them no matter how much they disagree with who they are. Stop making excuses as to why you can't accept your child's 'lifestyle'. My child didn't choose to be who she is and it's not a 'lifestyle'. A lifestyle is choosing to take trips to Miami for summer vacations, being who you are isn't. No mother should ever turn her back on her child. The world is a cold, hard place for children who are different and no matter how old our children get they need us. So, love your child no matter what. Be happy that they have the courage to be honest with who they are. Too many of these kids are out there alone, with no one to turn to.

I also want people to understand that when they hurt these kids they hurt everyone who love them. What those men did could have killed my child and all because she chose to be who she is. Stop killing our children. How many times must I pack up and move? Why should my child not be left alone to be herself? Stop hiding behind religion and everything else. My Renae was not "converted" by anyone and she didn't choose to be a lesbian either. I knew she was different since she was a small child. I watched her grow into herself.

^^^^^

Dana

The male police officer led me into a room and offered me a cup of water. He left and said someone would be there to help me shortly. Not long after, I heard whispering outside the door and a female officer entered. Still, I did not know what to say. They had turned me away from the emergency room telling me that in order for them to do a rape kit I needed to go report *it* to the police and they would take me back to be seen. Both shock and anger filled me because I couldn't understand why the nurse wouldn't help me. She had a duty of care, I needed medical attention. It took setting aside all my pride to tell the nurse those few words and now she was asking me to go tell someone else. I sat in the police station unable to say anything to the policewoman now sitting across from me.

"Do you want me to leave and come back after a while?" she had asked me, but I still couldn't respond to her.

She reached out her hand, and without contributing consciously to my reaction, I pulled back and fell over with the chair.

"Oh no!" she yelled and tried to help me but my emotions came in a flood and everything that had happened in the last few hours came rushing to the surface. I curled up into a ball at her feet. She yelled out for help, *"Chief! Come in here!"*

"Why is she on the floor?!" he asked.

"She fell. She's bleeding but I can't tell where the wound is."

"Young lady, get up so we can assess you."

His voice pierced through me and I was screaming at the top of my lungs. I know they were talking but I couldn't hear them anymore. The pain seemed real, as though it was happening all over again right there with them in the room.

After what seemed like a long time, I was sat with the female officer again trying to tell her what happened. The cut under my left breast wasn't fatal according to her, and it would soon all be looked over at the hospital. But the cut and other bruises were the least of my worries. Somehow, I had come back to my senses and I was angry with myself for being in the room. I was unsure as to how I was going to tell her what transpired without telling her the full story. As the thoughts of her shunning me the moment I told her the truth ran through my mind I began to sob.

"I just need to go to the hospital and be seen. Can you go with me? The nurse said the police has to come."

"Why did they ask for the police? What happened to you? Were you raped?

"No!"

She looked puzzled, "then why do you need the police?"

"All I want is to see the doctor!"

"Okay, calm down now. If you tell me what happened then I can take you back to the hospital."

"Ma'am, nothing happened. I need to see a doctor."

"Why do you need to see the doctor?"

"Because I'm bleeding, I need stitches!" I was still sobbing.

"Do you have any other cuts other than the one I've seen?"

"Yes," I murmured under my breath.

"Did you say 'yes'?"

"I just want to go to the hospital!" I got up to leave but she got up and stood in front of the door.

"I'm trying to help you. Let's just sit and talk this through," she led me back to my chair.

"You want to help me because you don't know the truth. Once you do you will probably want to do this to me all over again! Just let me leave. I will figure it out."

"Dana, it's obvious that something has happened to you and if the nurse sent you here it's because you have been raped and that is a crime. If you tell me what happened then I can help you. My colleague and I will take you to the hospital so that you can get medical attention and we will explain the rest. But you

need to tell me what happened so that I can start the process. No one here will hurt you and no matter what you say to me this is not your fault. You can't be thinking that and I'm in no way shape or form thinking that."

Every single word she said registered because all I could think of was how she would take them all back one by one as soon as I told her the truth. I began to weep for myself. All I wanted to do was to go to the hospital to see to the cut and bruises and to get some form of injection or pill or whatever to prevent me getting some form of disease. Sitting there was driving me crazy because I didn't have to be there, I probably should've just called my father or my brother to help me and they would have been there. Then it occurred to me that I probably should call them.

"Can you please call my father for me? I don't have a phone."

"Does he know where you are?"

"No, he's in Kingston but if you call him he will come immediately."

"Okay, what's his number?"

I gave her the number but she didn't leave the room she kept asking me to tell her what had happened. She didn't want to call my father and not have answers for him was her excuse. I knew she was only trying to get it out of me. But I still couldn't. No one helps you if they know you are gay. She would call me a sodomite and whatever other degrading names she could come up with if she knew the truth.

*****

The pain was getting worse in the back of my neck. The bleeding had stopped under my breast but the pain there wasn't going anywhere. There was no feeling in my vagina as had been the case from the moment it all started.

I felt disconnected from it, as though it wasn't a part of me anymore. I kept wishing it wasn't; that somehow it had disappeared from under me.

"You can get your pen and paper, and remember I told you that all of this is pointless. But please promise me that you will take me back to the hospital to be looked after."

"I will take you to the hospital."

*****

About eleven weeks earlier I had met a girl called 'Ramona' on DigiChat. I was single and lonely and welcomed the attention. Before long I spent every moment of every day either thinking about her or chatting with her. I imagined it was the same for her, she had even professed her love on our chats. We talked about everything including the fact that we would want to be in a relationship with each other. The only hurdle was the fact that we hadn't met in person.

Two weeks ago, she was meant to visit but I waited at the bus station and she never showed up. At first, I was worried that something had happened on the way, but none of the drivers who came in on the same route had seen or heard of an accident. To add insult to injury, I couldn't reach her. So, after waiting for over four hours pass her expected arrival time, I decided to go back home.

Overnight, I had only my thoughts to plague me and for the first time I began to question our 'relationship' and everything that had gone on between us thus far. I'd never actually spoken to her on the phone, I didn't even know her actual phone number. All I had was a chat history from a private chat we had created, a first name and a few photos she'd sent me from her cousin's phone. Who knows if that was even her? I questioned this for the very first time.

95

I couldn't sleep. I replayed every moment since the time she'd said "hello" in my mind. Mixed emotions consumed me; was she okay? Did she ever plan on coming to see me? What could have possibly stopped her and why wasn't she answering my calls?

I'd had enough of going crazy out of my mind with worry and anger so hours earlier I'd stopped looking at the photographs of her, re-reading our messages and decided to turn the tv on. I could hear the notifications come in on the phone, but for some reason I thought the noise was coming from the tv. When I realised messages were coming in from her I was elated.

"hello sugar

sorry I didn't make it

you there??????? Hello!!!!!!

Angry?"

I didn't want to respond but I knew she would keep going until I eventually answered.

"Hi" I finally wrote back.

According to her, her sister's daughter had fallen ill. While she sat waiting for the bus to be fully boarded by passengers, her sister had called and asked her to go to the hospital with her. Her phone died on the way to the hospital and they spent the night there with her niece hence she wasn't able to get in touch with me until now.

I was relieved to hear from her and was understanding as I would have done the same for a family member but I was disappointed that she hadn't made it. She wouldn't get another weekend off until the next two weeks and I wanted to know where we were going with our relationship before then. I really liked her but was getting impatient. I wanted to be sure I wasn't wasting my time and energy.

She thought it was pointless that I come to visit her the following weekend because she wouldn't be home most of the time due to work and invited me to come see her on her next weekend off in two weeks. I was ecstatic. Nothing was going to get in the way of us meeting then; I would walk to her if it came to that but I was surely going to meet her in two weeks and that wasn't so far away. In no time, I would be face to face with her and our future would be laid out for us. It was going to be one of the most important days of our lives, of my life at least.

*****

Time seemed to have slowed down drastically; even stopped. A moment seemed like an hour; a day like a year. Seeing her seemed farther and farther away and I was getting impatient. But something began to worry me. Our chats began to change sometimes. It made me question whether it was Ramona on the other end. Something about the messages just seemed off sometimes. As though another person was writing them. Sometimes the spelling, the layout or even just the idiom was off. I asked her about this a few times but she assured me that she lived alone and no one at work had access to her phone. Her explanation never sat well with me. It remained in my subconscious and I couldn't shake it.

The Monday of the week I was meant to go see her she came up with some stupid excuse about her house not being 'all that' and suggested I might want to stay at a hotel. I found it quite strange.

"You live there so I'm sure I will like it.".

"yeah you can say that now
when you get here you won't want to stay"

"Mona, I want to visit you in your home or you come to mine. If we decide to be in a relationship are you planning to move to a new place?"

99

"What?

Why do you ask that?

Of course, not"

"My point exactly. Hence, I'm visiting you at your house or you mine. I want to be a part of everything that you are not just some of it.

I want to see the bed you lay in at nights to send me all these sweet messages and everything else ☺."

"Look at you!

Hahahahahaha

Fine ... remember I said you won't like it"

"I will love it."

Thursday of that week finally came. One more day before I see her. I was beginning to feel nervous. What if she doesn't like me in person? What if I don't like her, what then? I packed and repacked my bag a million times trying to make sure I packed the *right* things but nothing seemed right. I wanted to impress her. Would this shirt match this pair of pants well enough? Will she even like my style? I must have paired up my clothes a thousand times trying to get it *right* and I still felt I couldn't. Eventually I decided to focus on my chat with her. But once again it happened.

Ramona had a specific way of saying things. She texted as though she thought only a few words at a time. We were the opposite. She rarely ever made full sentences; she only did if she was trying to explain a problem she had at work, this was the only time. But a message came in and it was a full sentence about looking forward to seeing me and laced with grammatical errors. I didn't respond and another message didn't follow. When I asked her about the message the following morning she took a few minutes to respond to it then said it was her who sent it. I was suspicious.

*****

Friday was finally here. At work, I was anxious I kept making simple mistakes. My colleagues caught me daydreaming a few times. My thoughts were all over the place, but I couldn't wait to see her. Something inside me was making me very unsettled though. We barely talked throughout the day as was the case when I was at work. But at lunch time she expressed her excitement and told me of the preparations she was making to ensure I was comfortable on my visit. She was also going to be making my favourite meal: ackee and salt-fish with boiled green bananas and she promised to crush the bananas for me. I was a peculiar eater and she didn't seem to mind.

My work day ended and I grabbed the bag I had packed the night before from under my desk and made my way to the bus station. A friend rang while I sat waiting on the bus. She was outside my house; had popped in for a visit. I explained I was on my way to see Ramona and that I'd see her as soon as I returned. Mine was the shoulder my friend cried on when she was having a rough time and she needed me now but I was desperate to follow this through. She was understanding. Just before the bus drove off a friend from work rang to say that he had found my wallet under my desk. I was surprised. I swore I had it with me but after searching my person I realised I didn't. Unfortunately, this was the last bus down. We only needed two more passengers to leave so I wouldn't make it back in time. This was my only way to get to her. I found enough money in my pockets for the return trip and a bit extra so I asked him to hold on to my wallet until Monday.

"Don't max out my cards now," I had said jokingly.

The journey seemed long. Half the time I couldn't get any network service so I couldn't chat with Ramona as I wanted to. Soon the bus pulled into the station and I was shaking from anxiety. I tried looking for her out the window but I couldn't see her. I sent her a message asking her where she was and it was only then that she said her cousin Raymond was picking me up instead. I didn't like the idea but she explained that he has a car and he would take me directly to her house. I'd never heard of Raymond before but I was there now and there was not much I could do at that point.

Raymond appeared just outside the bus station in a white Toyota Camry. He had dreads and for some reason that made me feel more relaxed about going on this journey with him. He seemed pleasant, reserved but pleasant. He explained that he drives a taxi on the route to his cousin's house and that chances are he might pick up people on the way. He didn't have a taxi licence plate on the car but that didn't surprise me as this sort of hustle was common.

Less than 10 mins up the road he picked up what seemed like a girl in her teens wearing a pair of very short denim shorts covered in writing of different colours and a red merino with a marijuana leaf in the centre. She wore a red 27-piece weave and spoke in a vulgar manner as she entered the car. They seemed familiar which wasn't strange for passengers and taxi drivers. I messaged Ramona again but got no response. Raymond's phone went off and he relayed the message that Ramona had supposedly sent him explaining that she couldn't get into chat now but she'll see me soon. 'Weird,' I thought, 'she could've used the same time to send me a message telling me that.'

Moments later, Raymond stopped and two men got into the car. One sat behind me and the other behind Raymond. The unsettlement, I had been feeling all day began to worsen. I sent Ramona a few more chats but I soon noticed that every time my chat message went through Raymond's phone gave an alert that a message or something had come through. Panic took over and I tried hard not to let it show on my face.

"How much further do we have to go?" I asked him.

"It's not that far but we still have to get out of town."

"I'm desperate to use the toilet is there any close by?"

"Well if you can afford to hold it a bit longer and don't mind peeing in the bush then yes otherwise you will have to wait until you get to Ramona's."

"The bush is fine!" I blurted out. All ideas of meeting Ramona had disappeared at the sound of my messages coming through on Raymond's phone. So, by some means, I needed this car to stop and I needed to find a way out of this. I was not going to let them take me to a house where I was unsure of what would happen to me or whether I would come out alive.

"So, you're a lesbian then?" the girl in the back questioned.

"Why do you say that?" I asked.

"It's obvious. Look at the way you dress."

The men began to laugh. Then Raymond butted in, *"no disrespect still but the I don't like Babylon things so I hope you're as straight as an arrow."*

"I am. I have my baby father and three children at home." I was lying through my teeth but something inside reminded me that they knew the truth.

"Are you sure though?" she asked. *"You just look like one of them."*

"Yes, very sure."

"Okay, so you think 'those kind of people' deserve to live free in this place?" she continued with the invasion.

"What do you mean?"

"Like walk around free like everybody else spreading their disease and corrupting other people. You lesbians need a good dick and all battyman must be shot in the head, execution....."

"*Come on,*" I interrupted, "*I don't think it's your right or mine to judge anyone. As a matter of fact….*"

The man sat behind me interrupted, "*why does it sound like you're getting defensive?*"

"*I was just thinking the same thing,*" Raymond added. "*You sound like you believe in this Eve and Eve fuckeries.*"

"*It's not a matter of being defensive,*" I could feel myself getting angry now, "*I just don't agree with us sitting here casting judgement and worse of all saying people should be killed for not being straight.*"

"*Well that's being defensive.*" Raymond said.

I sucked my teeth in annoyance, "*say what you will. Anyway, remember to stop so I can relieve myself.*"

The three in the back began to talk about who's right it was to set a lesbian straight. It was shocking to hear the girl saying all the vile things she said. In her opinion, all a lesbian needed was to be shown how to be a woman; "to submit to the rod of correction" was how she'd put it.

I began to plan my escape. As soon as the car stopped I would run into the bushes and hopefully they wouldn't follow and if they did I would run with all my might until they got fed up and stopped. The car began to slow down. My plan was about to be put to the test. But the guy who sat behind me got out before the car came to a complete stop. When we stopped he opened my door. Soon they all got out and formed a semi-circle around me.

"We'll block you off from the road," the girl said.

"No, it's okay, I can just go into the bush a little bit. It's....."

"No, we will block you. Piss right here." Raymond ordered.

I succumbed. My plan wasn't fool proof anyway and they would have outran me as soon as I took off. I felt defeated. But I knew I needed a way out. I forced myself to pee then I unwillingly got back into the car with them and we continued on our way.

"Raymond, you and Ramona are cousins on which side of the family, your mother or father?"

"Father," the girl responded.

And I was now very sure that they had plans for me I couldn't have foreseen through eleven weeks of chats.

"So, what's the plan?" The words escaped my lips.

"The plan?" she began to laugh uncontrollably, then finally leaned over and said to Raymond, *"you picked a smart one. She caught on real fast"*

I grabbed her in her weave and attempted to pull her to the front of the car. The man behind me caught me in a chokehold telling me to let go but I knew if I did that was it so I kept pulling and he kept choking me. Raymond soon slammed on the breaks and she was flung into the dashboard. The guy didn't let go, I barely jerked forward. He gripped my neck even tighter and I was choking. I began beating his arm but he didn't budge. I felt as though my brain was about to explode through my temple and tears began flowing out of my eyes, I was choking.

Finally, Raymond shouted at him, *"Bolo, release her! Let her go!"*

When he finally did I felt my behind meet the car seat. I couldn't stop coughing. Soon I was being dragged by my shirt into the bushes by feet. I kept screaming asking them to leave me alone and all the time the girl was telling me to shut up. She pushed me to the ground and I felt a stab beneath my left breast. Something was lodged in the wound. One of the men took off my shoes and then my pants. It was a scuffle, I tried to pull away but I was pulled back by my legs and soon they had succeeded.

"Stop, this. Let's just leave her and go." The guy who sat behind Raymond said.

"Shut up," she screamed, *"all of a sudden you have a fucking change of heart, pussy!"*

"Yow chill. He's right. This isn't right. Let's go." Raymond said.

"Come Bolo, this bitch can't leave like this. These fucking pussies. She'll bring the police. Do you really think we can let her go now?"

"She's right, we have to do this." Bolo said.

"No, I won't bring the police, I promise. Please, just let me go. No one will know."

"Bolo, this is wrong man. I can't be witness to this. Let her go. She doesn't even know any of us. She can't….."

"Raymond is right!" I quickly interjected, *"I don't know any of you. Please don't hurt me anymore. I won't come back. I don't even live close to this place. No one will ever know"*

"Nooooooo!!!!!" she demanded, *"Raymond is a coward! And don't tell us not to do this as if we planned it. Let's finish this! Bolo, your turn first."*

"I'll do my part because I'm not going to prison for anyone. If we let her go we are all fucked!" Bolo said.

113

"I'll wait in the car." The man with no name said.

"Do you pussy! You fucking son of a bitch!" she yelled at him. *"Bitch open your legs."*

I was covering my vagina with my hands, lying on the ground, the three of them now surrounding me; looking at me with scorn, but I could also see the fear. When I didn't open my legs, she kicked me and I was lucky that my hand was covering my vagina otherwise it would have been more painful. I fanned my hand to relieve the pain. Bolo was standing with his pants around his ankles. She kicked me again and I decided that it was better to give them what they wanted. It was going to go on for as long as I wanted it to. The more I resisted the longer it would take and the worse it would be. Their minds were made up. They were there to do a job and as she said they were going to carry it out.

I stared into the dark skies above me, not a star in sight. Bolo climbed atop me, I felt his bare skin touching mine. I escaped my body, zoned out. I didn't cry. I couldn't give them that satisfaction. I felt as stiff as the dead. When he was done, the girl stood over me. A metal rod in her hand. She pressed her foot into my abdomen. She bent over me and pressed the cold iron between my thighs and it brought me back to reality. The reality was, if I didn't fight for my life they were going to take it. She had said it as plain as day and I couldn't just give in. I felt a kind of unbelievable strength rise up inside of me and I grabbed the metal rod from her and whacked her over the head with. No sooner did she fall to the ground than I had grabbed my pants and ran into the bushes; into the unknown.

They must've had to help her because no one came after me. I didn't know where I was or where I was going. But I kept running. I came up on a river and was eager to cleanse myself but something told me not to. Something

115

was still lodged below my left breast; I finally pulled my attention to it. It was a small piece of glass bottle and it wasn't that deep in so I pulled it out. I pressed on the wound to control the bleeding. I drank from the river and washed my face. I desperately searched my pocket and found that my money was still intact, my phone was missing.

I sat by the river giving thanks that I was alive and that by some means I could get back home. But it wasn't long before pain and worry started to set in and I knew I needed to make it to a hospital. There were no houses in sight. Bushes surrounded me. I decided to follow the river downstream. After walking for what seemed like hours I had still not seen civilization, so I decided to take a break, I was almost out of breath. I kept taking breaks until I had hit a bridge that connected two roads above me.

Soon people were everywhere. I tried to hide my scars and my pain. A gentleman offered to take me to the hospital but I couldn't get into another car with another unknown man. It soon occurred to me that I needed to get off the streets because Raymond and his friends were probably looking for me.

I made it to the hospital and sat in the emergency unit waiting to be seen by a doctor. The sun came up and I was still waiting. Finally, when a nurse saw me I was told I needed to go to the police station straight from there before they could examine me. We debated but I wasn't winning. I had to go to the police station, so I made my way there.

*****

I wasn't prepared to tell the police any of this. We all know how it ends. They can't even help little girls and women who are straight and raped or molested; and it is well known that the police do absolutely nothing to help gay people even when they see the injustice with their own two eyes. So, I gave her a story that would get me to the hospital and she kept her promise.

^^^^^

Carla

Until now I didn't intend to share this with anyone. I still feel shame and self-resentment because somehow, I know that I brought it on myself. It could have all been prevented; no matter how I try to make sense of it I think to myself, that if only I had the courage things wouldn't have turned out the way they did.

Back in high-school all the girls were dating boys and I felt I had no choice but to do the same. There were girls I liked sexually and liking boys just didn't come naturally. After being boyfriend free up to grade eleven, I started dating a boy named Johnny who was friends with my best friend's boyfriend. Being gay wasn't an option; everyone was homophobic and I wasn't about to be treated differently. I wanted to be accepted by my friends and everyone else more than I wanted to be myself.

Johnny and I remained in a relationship until long after high school and we kept breaking up and making up for years before it finally came to an end. I got a job as a waitress, it wasn't my dream job but I got the job and it was paying the bills and so I got comfortable and soon forgot about my dreams of saving and going off to college. Johnny managed to pool some money together to buy a car and went into the taxi business so it was him who picked me up to take me to work and back every single day even when we were at war and no longer 'in a relationship'.

Most of our fights had to do with my inability to commit and play house with him. At 23, Johnny was ready to be a father and have a family with a woman to come home to, but I knew I couldn't do that. I couldn't be that for him. I didn't want to be a mother and I knew I didn't feel for him what I was supposed to. I stayed with him because I 'needed to have a boyfriend' to appease everyone, and even though I loved him as a person I didn't love him in

120

that way. Having sex with him was the most stressful part of my life but every so often and to keep him from complaining as much as he did, I would give in. Even then he would complain because according to him I was boring in bed, lifeless. I wanted to let him go so that he could find someone to give him what he wanted, but I was selfish. I just didn't want the stigma to follow me for one second. I didn't want any attention drawn to who I really was. I'd seen how different people around me were treated for being gay or not conforming to their gender and I didn't want to go through any of it. Plus, I wasn't going to get into it with another man who might be more difficult and demanding than he was.

*****

Secretly, I was having relations with women. Since graduating I had met different girls at work and had flings with them. None lasted long because they would want to meet or talk outside of work and fooling around in the bathroom stalls and then cutting them off was all I was interested in. I tried my best to keep it out of my personal life, but it soon caught up with me.

A group of girls came into the restaurant one evening just before my shift ended and it was obvious they were lesbians. They didn't try to hide it. Somehow, they knew I was one of them and they were far from discrete.

"Family," one of the women said loud enough for everyone in the restaurant to look at her.

Not wanting to make it obvious she was referring to me I stared just like everyone else. They all giggled and everyone seemed annoyed with the group. I wanted them to leave, my shift couldn't end soon enough. I could see Amira eyeballing me from across the restaurant. We had just broken off our fling and she had cussed me out the worse possible way, telling me that the only person I was hiding from was myself. According to her 'even a blind man could tell I was a dyke'

That incident drove fear into me and I decided to put that part of me aside. I tried to walk the straight and narrow. The opportunities to have a one-night stand with a girl kept coming and I kept refusing and the restaurant was churning out dykes like it was Christmas. Other than myself and two other guys, no one was staying on. They were getting fired sooner than they were hired and it was one lesbian or bisexual woman after the next. It was as though God was playing tricks on me. But I kept suppressing my feelings and refused the advances that came.

Trouble came walking in like food being dangled in front of a starving man. In walked my high school crush one fine day in the middle of my shift, and it stopped me in my tracks.

"Oh my God, Shaky is that you?"

"What's up mami?" she spoke with an American accent, *"it's been forever, how you doin'?"*

"Is that a twang I hear? Where have you been?" I was draped over her now and we held each other for longer than a moment.

She got the name Shaky because she had such a huge ass that it 'shook' when she moved. Every boy and girl wanted to be with her or like her back then and looking at her now in front of me I doubted that fact had changed. She was drop dead gorgeous, just plain beautiful and she was smart too. I hadn't seen her since graduation. It started all over again. We exchanged numbers.

*****

Raquel (Shaky) and I rekindled our friendship over the next few weeks. We caught up on each other's lives and it was as though we had never missed a beat. We stopped being friends back in the start of the eleventh grade because I couldn't handle being around her constantly. I was in love and I didn't want it to be known so I started avoiding her and eventually we stopped talking. I missed our friendship and we had missed out on so much. She was living in Chicago now and was only visiting for the summer. We spent most of the summer together and I didn't dare let her know how I felt about her. When we said goodbye at the airport we both cried but for me it was more than saying goodbye to a friend; I cried for all that would just never be.

We talked every day over the next few months and I forgot to pay attention to Johnny and he was noticing and complaining as usual so I broke it off with him for the umpteenth time. I wasn't sure how Raquel felt about me though. She was also in a relationship; engaged, and as far as I could tell she was in love with her fiancé. It was confusing because she called and texted as though we were in a relationship and if I didn't respond to her text quick enough she'd be upset with me. So, I finally decided to face my fears and asked her what's up.

"Have you ever been with a girl before?'

"What? Why do you ask that?"

"I'm just asking. Have I offended you?" the line went quiet for a few seconds.

"I know you're not on that trip, I still remember how homophobic you and your new friends were, and I'm not on it either."

"Woah, you think I'm homophobic, like really?"

"We both know you are."

"Wow, okay if that's what you think then I guess that's what it is," I wasn't sure what to make of it. I wasn't sure what was going on between us either and I needed a quick escape from this conversation. *"I have to go hon."* I hung up without waiting for her response.

She rang back immediately.

"Why did you hang up the phone? That was a bit rude."

"It just got cut off," I lied.

"No, it didn't, you hung up. Why do you sound like you're crying?"

"I'm not crying," I lied again.

"You're making me concerned now. You dropped this question on me, hung up the phone and now you're crying. What's up Boo?"

127

"I'm good. I really have to go now."

"Why don't you just talk to me, be straight with me please. Just be open."

"What makes you think I'm not being straight with you? What do you mean by that? Is there something you want to say?"

"I'm just saying I don't understand what's going on."

"I really have to go, I'm going to hang up the phone now. I love you. Enjoy the rest of your day." I hung up.

*****

Over the next few weeks I tried hard to avoid the topic and eventually she'd stopped asking what that was about. I was still unsure as to what was going on between us. Johnny and I got back together the same night that I had that 'talk' with Raquel. I wanted to just forget about what I was feeling for her so unfairly I turned to him for comfort and as usual we made up and were in a relationship that was going nowhere again. We started having sex more often and I began to realise that it was to make up for the fact that I couldn't be with Raquel. Whenever, I got frustrated and couldn't deal with what felt like a loss anymore I would find myself in Johnny's bed. He noticed that I had changed too. Said I seemed less present but I was more involved. I knew why; I was thinking of her while I was with him

I tried to limit the time I gave to Raquel because I wasn't sure if she was playing with my feelings or just completely oblivious to the fact that I was in love with her. I missed her every second of everyday and the more I stayed away from her the more I wanted her. She constantly complained of me trying to distance myself and I felt guilty for not being there at her disposal because she took all my calls and my messages as usual.

In the middle of scrolling through her MySpace account lusting over her, my brother knocked at my bedroom door to let me know that someone was outside to see me. I was surprised because I wasn't expecting anyone. It was her. She was standing in our living room. It was a beautiful surprise and I cried.

"Aren't you happy to see me?" she wiped the tears from my eyes while I still clung to her.

"I'm more than happy." I almost kissed her but I caught myself just in time.

She visited for two weeks and we spent every moment we could together. On about the third day I spent the night at her hotel and we made love for the first time. It was her who initiated it and it was then that we decided that we wanted to be together. She had already ended it with her fiancé the moment she had returned from her summer trip without telling me and she wanted me to end it with Johnny. I wanted to be with her but I was terrified.

I wasn't ready for this and she wasn't just talking about us

fooling around she wanted a real-life relationship. She

wanted it to just be us. I promised to break up with Johnny

when she was gone. He wasn't doing anything that would

give me a reason to break it off with him and I didn't want

him putting it all together. One evening after work when I

asked Johnny to drop me at her hotel, he jokingly said he

was a fool for dropping me off to see my 'spare tyre', hence

I knew I needed to be very careful. But, as the saying goes,

'where there is smoke there is fire' and boy was there fire.

Raquel came over to spend time with my mother as

she was leaving in a couple of days. She adored my mother

so she made seeing her priority. I was going to be spending

the next two days at her hotel with her and I was looking

forward to it. I told Johnny I was going to stay with her

and he offered to pick us up and take us to the hotel later

that night and I agreed. Raquel was not happy with my

decision but I thought it best not to argue with her or cancel because I didn't want to fuss with her or him.

Johnny arrived at my house with our friend Marcus who we had gone to high school with as well. He was still wearing his mechanic clothes covered in grease.

"What's up Shaky, everything good." he didn't seem too surprised to see her.

"It's been a minute," she smiled, *"I'm good. What's up with you?"*

"It's all good. Hustling as usual, making a living."

"Marcus, Marcus, Marcus, I can't believe I'm laying eyes on you. Do you remember how you used to chase me around the school yard trying to kiss me?"

He gave his usual cheeky giggle, *"Yes I do, and I still never got a kiss from you."*

"That's because you were busy chasing every skirt you could. How many babies and baby mama's do you have?"

132

"I'm a good youth. I don't roll like that," smiling and licking his lips.

"Tell the truth," I butted into the conversation.

"Stay out of the conversation!" Johnny growled.

"What's your problem Johnny," I was puzzled, it was as though we were having an argument, *"why are you angry?*

He hissed his teeth and pretended I wasn't talking to him.

"You know what, let me leave you grown folks. Raquel, I'll get the bags. You can get into the car."

"No wait up for me," she followed me, *"I still need to say goodbye to your mother properly."*

I knew she didn't want to say goodbye to my mom, she already did and my mom was already sleeping which she knew.

133

"Boo, what was that about," she whispered, "why is he being so aggressive?"

"I really don't know what his problem is. Now I don't even want to get into his stupid car with him and his stupidity."

"It's cool, just ignore him. Let's not cause a scene. Maybe he's having a bad day. He's just dropping us off anyway so let him do that. You'll be leaving his ass sooner than he thinks and you won't have to deal with him anymore."

"This is why I need to get my own damn car, I cannot deal with his constant bullshit!"

"Soon you won't have to, let's go."

Marcus and Raquel were busy reminiscing on school days and I sat in the back of the car not saying a word. I didn't want to get into a fight with Johnny. He wanted to drop something off for a friend in Constant Spring and they agreed amongst themselves that he was going to do this before dropping us at the hotel. Like I said, I didn't want to argue so even though I didn't want to go I didn't protest.

We came up to a gate with two men standing outside; they seemed to be expecting us. The men got out of the car and huddled together. I couldn't hear their conversation because I was now having a fight with Raquel for agreeing to come here. Johnny soon disrupted our little fight when he came to the car to say that they were going inside and we should go with them because it was going to be a while.

"It's okay, we can wait here for you."

"Two women can't just sit here in this neighbourhood, come with me. I'll try to make it quick."

"Johnny, do your thing and let's go but I don't want to go into the house. I don't even know these guys."

He raised his voice, *"Carla, why do you always have to be a problem? Get the hell out of the car and let's go."*

Raquel signalled for me to go with him and I obliged. She followed behind me.

The house looked as though it was not occupied. There was no veranda so we went into what seemed like a makeshift living room/bedroom. The four men went into the other room which had a door on it and locked it behind them. Johnny came out a while after and said he wanted to talk with me outside. He told Raquel to stay behind. We got outside but he said nothing and after asking him over and over again I attempted to go back inside but he stopped me.

"Are you fucking Raquel?"

"Are you crazy! Why..."

"Don't take me for an idiot!" he was irate. *"As a matter of fact, don't answer the question. Now I know for a fact that you are. And all this while, you've been playing me, taking me for a dickhead."*

"Johnny, that's crazy talk. We are just friends. That's all, I swear."

"And what if I ask her? What then? Are you still going to look me in the eye and deny it?"

"Why would you want to embarrass me like that? You're not just saying I'm cheating on you but that I'm cheating with a woman? Stop talking crazy!" I tried to make sure I wasn't sounding condescending.

"Exactly my point. You're a wicked woman and, don't even raise your voice at me," he was speaking in his very low voice almost pensive, *"you are fucking Raquel. You've been taking me for a dickhead making me look like a fool in front of everyone."*

"Can you stop accusing me!"

"Let me just make this clear, whatever the two of you have going on, is about to come to an end."

"What do you mean by that? We are just friends!"

"You aren't fooling anyone, especially not me, so stop denying it. And this lesbian business will stop after today." He ushered me back in.

I entered the house to find Raquel kneeling on the floor in what seemed like her urine and one of the men was holding a gun to her head. The rest is history.

*****

We were both raped and forced to perform oral sex while Johnny watched. We were submissive because we wanted to live. When they were done they made us promise on our lives not to tell anyone and so we did.

Johnny dropped Raquel at her hotel but I had to go home with him and for me it didn't end. As sore and bruised as I was, he still forced me to have sex with him over and over and over again that night. He didn't allow me to sleep a wink.

^^^^^

Abba

When Kev turned up that evening asking me to make a quick run with him into town I didn't think anything of it as this was common. He was my best friend. He knew me better than anyone else. We both had strong personalities that often clashed but we would always work out our issues. We loved each other like family. He was the first person for me to come out to back in high school and he never treated me differently. He often stood up for me and got into a few fist fights when people attacked my sexuality. We knew each other since we were seven in Sunday School. To a lot of people, he had a crush on me but I never saw it. We were like two brothers, and even if I was straight I'd never think of us together because he was like family and he seemed to have felt the same way.

On the drive, we chatted about random stuff including our plan to go out "skirt chasing" that weekend. We had plans to go visit a friend in Montego Bay where we'd spend our time going to a couple of house parties and a big road dance and we were both looking forward to it. He stopped at his gate.

"Aren't we going into town?"

"Yeah man, I just want to show you something first," he suddenly seemed nervous.

In my mind, it could have been anything; a new video game, a new pair of shoes, a rare insect he had found in his garden anything except this. His room was set up for romance and I was beside myself when he said it was all for me.

141

"Hahahahahahahaha," I was laughing hysterically, "*dude, be serious are you having someone over? On a serious note, it's a lot of effort and you're sure to 'get some' from her.*"

He was not amused, "*I do all this for you and you're laughing in my face?*"

"*Hold on a minute, you are serious. Dude are you for real? We are the same, you and me. I like pussy as much as you do maybe even more and I definitely don't do dicks.*" I was still amused and still couldn't put on a stern face.

"*I'm just messing with you,*" he was laughing now, "*I'm having a little visit later.*"

"*Dude you freaked me the fuck out! But hold on a minute, why is it that this is the first time I'm hearing about it?*"

"*It's a spur of the moment thing man. Nothing too serious.*"

"All this for something that's not so serious? It sure is going to get serious tonight with all these candles and shit. These girls out here really like this shit. I need to take a page out of your book."

"That you do, maybe then you will keep a woman."

"That's not funny," we were both laughing, *"maybe if I slowed down a bit they would stay."*

"Let's have a beer before I drop you off."

We went into his backyard with a six pack and I pulled up two crates for us to sit on. I remember getting blurred vision and feeling light headed only after the first few sips. I was a heavy drinker so I knew something wasn't right with the drink he gave me but it was too late and whatever he had put in it was fast acting. I was out cold.

I don't remember most of the first night because I kept going in and out of consciousness. I have slight

143

memories of feeling discomfort in my vagina and feeling the weight of his body on top of me but it's all a blur.

I came to and my naked body was tied to his bed; my legs and arms spread and tied to the bed posts. Still feeling light headed I tried to free myself but with the grip of the restraints it was impossible. I could barely move my limbs. I was gagged so it was also impossible to call for help. He was nowhere in sight and I assumed he must've left me there to go to work. Later he returned and it was like coming home to his wife rather than his captive. I felt betrayed but angry more than anything. I could've killed him with my bare hands and not felt an ounce of pain or remorse laying eyes on him.

He got a basin with water, a rag and bar of soap and sat next to me on the bed. I thought of how many ways I was going to make him pay while he cleaned my body. When he was done he removed the gag.

"What the fuck are you doing? Have you lost your God damn mind!?"

"Shhhhhh, I don't want to have to put this back." he showed me the cloth he'd just removed from my mouth.

"Are you fucking sick or what? Why the fuck are you doing this? Untie me! I'm going to kill you!"

"It's easy for me to just put this back so please be quiet, you need to eat something."

I couldn't believe what I was hearing, he sounded like a psychopath, *"Kev, untie me. I need to use the bathroom. You left me here all fucking day like this, I need to use the bathroom and give me my fucking clothes. You sick fuck!"*

"I'm sick? Are you kidding me? You're the one who is sick, thinking its normal to be fucking women and then telling me all about it. That's what's sick, you cunt! I've had to put up with you for all these years and I've had enough. You can be fixed. All of this is to fix you."

145

I was baffled. How did I not see this coming? We had done everything together almost all our lives and all of a sudden he had a problem with me and who I was; had someone taken over my best friend's body or what? None of this was making sense. This wasn't him. He was like a brother to me. This was beyond anything I could have ever imagined would ever unfold for us. I was flabbergasted. Why did it have to come to this and why now?

He fed me food forcefully. I'd refused to eat it because I suspected it was laced with whatever he had put in my beer and I was right. I was in and out of consciousness again and that night I felt the weight of his body on top of me and uninvited pressure in my vagina and of course I was in no position to refuse him. And this went on for the next three days; like a broken record replaying.

Just like that I woke up on the fourth morning and the ropes tying me to the bed were removed and I was dressed in a t-shirt and a pair of shorts I'd left at his house. He was nowhere to be found. I was filled with rage I took it out on his house. I tore it apart, all of it. I walked the entire neighbourhood looking for him and no one knew where he was, my phone was missing so I couldn't call the bastard. I hid in the vacant lot next door waiting for him to come home that evening to get my revenge but he never did. He never came home or back to the community.

I never told anyone because I was too ashamed and embarrassed. I was disgusted with the whole thing and didn't want anyone to know that it had happened. I moved away from the neighbourhood just to get away from it completely but of course that's not possible.

∧∧∧∧∧

Pat

The party wasn't over, but I left early because my knee was giving me hell. I left my girl with our friends because she was having so much fun. I didn't want to take that from her. Pulling up to our gate I noticed two men coming towards my car. I assumed they would continue on their merry way. It was almost 2AM but this wasn't suspicious. They appeared to be two men going about their business. Trying to make a right turn into the yard it was foreseeable they would either wait or walk in the street to get around me, but only one of them went into the street. The other seemed to be waiting for me to finish the maneuver; or so I thought.

"Yow, what are you doing?" I was addressing the man opening the passenger door.

In a split second the other man rushed to my side of the car. In a panic, I floored the gas and headed straight into the wall. I hurried to get the airbag out of my face and jumped out of the car. "I wasn't going to run either it was about to be a fist fight and I would take them both on", I told myself. Soon I realised that the one who had tried climbing into the passenger's seat was now lying flat on the ground groaning so immediately I thought "the playing field is more levelled".

My mother and daughter were inside the house but neither of them came out after the crash, none of the neighbours did either. I imagined people were asleep but could everyone be sleeping so soundly? I began to shout for help.

The other man was just standing there by my gate as if he was waiting to see my reaction. He stood smoking his cigarette; he looked fearless. "Worst case scenario, he has a gun, either way he was probably going to kill me whether I fought back or not so I might as well fight," I rationalized. I was used to getting into fights. I grew up with two brothers and I knew how to defend myself. They were always getting into trouble and had both been to prison so I assumed one or both of them had done something to warrant this current situation.

He began to walk into the yard and adrenaline kicked in. There was no way I was going to allow him to get to my family so I went after him. Catching up I swung at him but even with his back turned to me, he ducked just in time to miss the blow. He kicked me in my bad knee and I stumbled to the ground balancing on my good knee and arms.

"What do you want?!"

He struck me again, this time with a thump to the head. I fell on my back. I cried out for help again, this time for my mother. He came over me and forced his foot into my neck, it felt like a tonne of bricks were pressing me into the ground. When I stopped struggling he released me. And it wasn't long that he was joined by others, I couldn't count them. I stood to my feet. I went for the guy who I was fighting with disregarding their presence. I got a punch in just before he kicked me in my stomach causing me to cringe for a split second.

"Oh! You want to fight like a man, I'll fight you like a man then," he punched me again in my face this time my head spun to the other side and for a few moments I saw all white.

"What have I done?" I demanded. *"What have I done?"*

I felt a foot in my lower back that brought me again to my knees and in the same instant a blade passed over my right cheek and there was blood streaming down my face like a tap had been turned on. I couldn't feel any pain but I knew for sure he had cut me, he must have done something to the blade that prevented my flesh from sensing the injury. I struggled to my feet and tackled him to the ground.

"Argh!" I growled in agony.

Someone bent my right arm behind my back and hauled me off him.

"She doesn't seem to be giving up easily," one man announced.

"Let's make it quick, we've been here long enough," another added.

"Please, I have my daughter. What did I do to you, what did I do?"

"Were you thinking of your daughter while you were busy flaunting your dirty lifestyle around for everyone to see?" he questioned in disgust.

I knew then why they were there. I got myself in this mess by being myself. Everyone always assumed I was a lesbian but their assumptions were only confirmed recently when my girlfriend moved in to live with us. I guess it was obvious that we weren't 'just friends' and she wasn't a relative. At that very moment, I knew I was in far more trouble than I had originally thought. They will not leave me alive; not if they have a choice. I could not give up without a fight.

"Somebody help me! Hel...."

The man who was there first tried to stab me and one of the others stopped him. *"Boss man, we can't fuck a corpse. Hold off on that."*

Hearing this I stepped on the foot of the man holding me with all the strength I could and when he released his grip I turned around to run towards the gate. I almost reached the man standing by the gate seemingly on watch, when what felt like a brick knocked me to the ground. I was helpless now. I felt something crack in my lower back and I couldn't turn myself over. I was lying face down in our front yard screaming in pain and still the neighbourhood seemed to be asleep.

"Get up!"

"I can't, just do what you came here to do. Just finish and kill me." I heard myself say. I couldn't move, I tried but the discomfort was unbearable in my lower back.

"Move her, it looks like she really can't move. I think you broke her back."

"Serve her right, she must really think she's a man," he shrugged and obliged the orders by pulling me by my feet to the side of my house.

With my feet raised the pain was more agonizing. I was covered in my own blood, forced against the side of the house my pants had been cut off. They ripped off my shirt, the buttons spread out in different directions. My body was soon completely exposed and they laughed among themselves. They pulled my breast and attacked them with their mouths all the time I was recoiling in disbelief. I had no more fight left in me.

The third man to take his turn had barely penetrated me when I heard the sirens. They seemed to have heard it too and they disappeared. I immediately felt gratitude, I was still alive and help was on the way.

*****

My mother heard the crash and called the police. She had to protect my daughter so they both hid inside in wait. My neighbour had also heard and after a few phone calls from different people, the police finally came to my rescue.

^^^^^

Epilogue

"It changes you. It takes things from you that you didn't even know you have." These were the words spoken by Dana when I interviewed her, and over the years I have witnessed how "it" has affected the lives of these women. I have seen how "it" continues to take control of their lives and unfortunately some just can't seem to come back from "it".

Some of these women continue to live meaningful lives and continue to beat the odds. Though none of them ever tackled the Justice System in Jamaica to fight for justice for themselves, they all took my advice and assistance to seek counselling and help. Unfortunately, the story did not end well for everyone.

In 2011 Renae committed suicide and Lashaun passed away in 2013 after her long battle with HIV. Carla now lives in America with Raquel where they are raising their adopted son together. For years Pat's daughter struggled with the post-traumatic stress and still suffers from anxiety. Therapy has helped Pat and her family but her daughter has been the one most affected and she still struggles the most.

Rape affects the lives of its victims, and lesbian and bisexual women around the world continue to suffer in silence. These are just some of the many stories out there.

Injustice against any human being is injustice against

humankind

TAMARiND HiLL
.PRESS

Lightning Source UK Ltd.
Milton Keynes UK
UKHW02f0813100818
327047UK00008B/308/P

9 781999 815295